CARRIE UNDERWOOD
BLOWN AWAY

www.carrieunderwood.fm • www.carrieunderwoodofficial.com
www.facebook.com/carrieunderwood • www.twitter.com/carrieunderwood

 Produced by
Alfred Music Publishing Co., Inc.
P.O. Box 10003
Van Nuys, CA 91410-0003
alfred.com

Printed in USA.

ISBN-10: 0-7390-9173-5
ISBN-13: 978-0-7390-9173-9

Management: Simon Fuller, Ann Edelblute; XIX Entertainment
Photography: Randee St. Nicholas
Stylist: Emma Trask
Makeup: Francesca Tolot
Hair: Enzo Angileri

 Alfred Cares. Contents printed on 100% recycled paper,
except pages 1-4 which are printed on 60% recycled paper.

CONTENTS

GOOD GIRL

Words and Music by
CARRIE UNDERWOOD, ASHLEY GORLEY
and CHRIS DeSTEFANO

Good Girl - 7 - 1

6

8

10

BLOWN AWAY

Words and Music by
JOSH KEAR and CHRIS TOMPKINS

Moderately bright ♩ = 140

Verse 1:

1. Dry light-ning cracks a-cross__ the skies.__

Those storm clouds gath-er in__ her eyes.__

14 *Chorus:*

Chorus:

TWO BLACK CADILLACS

Words and Music by
CARRIE UNDERWOOD,
JOSH KEAR and HILLARY LINDSEY

Moderately ♩ = 116

22

23

Two Black Cadillacs - 7 - 4

24

26

Repeat ad lib. and fade

Two Black Cadillacs - 7 - 7

SEE YOU AGAIN

Words and Music by
CARRIE UNDERWOOD,
DAVID HODGES and HILLARY LINDSEY

Gtr. tuned down 1/2 step:
⑥ = E♭ ③ = G♭
⑤ = A♭ ② = B♭
④ = D♭ ① = E♭

Moderate rock ♩ = 100

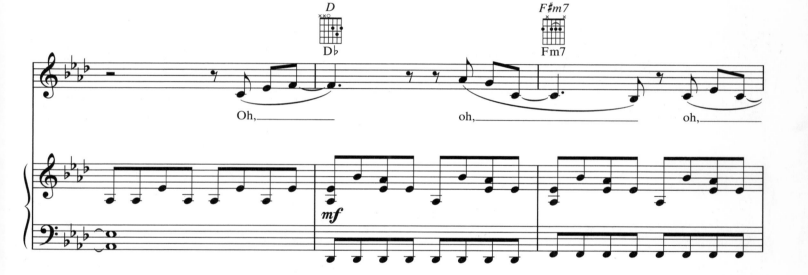

Oh,_____ oh,_____ oh,_____

_____ oh,_____ oh,_____ oh,_____

See You Again - 8 - 1

F#m7 A E
Fm7 A♭ E♭
oh, oh.
Verse 1 (sing 1st time only):
A5 F#m7
A♭5 Fm7
1. Said good-bye, turned a - round, and you were gone, gone, gone,
Verse 2 (sing 2nd time only):
2. I can hear those ech - oes in the wind at night
mp
D2 Esus
D♭2 E♭sus
fad - ed in - to the set - ting sun, slipped a - way.
call - ing me back in time, back to you

30

See You Again - 8 - 4

31

Bridge:

Some - times___ I feel my___ heart___ is___ break - ing. But

I stay strong___ and I hold___ on___ 'cuz I know..._____

See You Again - 8 - 5

32

DO YOU THINK ABOUT ME

Words and Music by
CARY BARLOWE, SHANE STEVENS
and HILLARY LINDSEY

* Original recording in D♭ major, guitars capo 1.

Do You Think About Me - 9 - 1

Do You Think About Me - 9 - 3

42

FOREVER CHANGED

Words and Music by
JAMES SLATER, TOM DOUGLAS
and HILLARY LINDSEY

Chorus 1:

Forever Changed - 8 - 2

46

Verse 2:

2. She re-mem-bers the change in her bod - y, the bloom-in' with - in, and how her___ heart___

Verse 3:

3. Some days she'll talk a - bout Aunt Ros - ie,

the sis-ter she lost, ask-ing___ when___ she's com-ing o - ver, and why she

has-n't called.___ Some days I just hold her frag-ile hand___ as time creeps 'cross the

floor.___ Some days___ it al-most kills___ me, watch-ing___ her mem-o - ry slip a-

50

51

Forever Changed - 8 - 8

NOBODY EVER TOLD YOU

Words and Music by
CARRIE UNDERWOOD,
LUKE LAIRD and HILLARY LINDSEY

Moderately ♩ = 96

Verse:

1. Take off all the make-up, girl, shine your light, show the world.
(2.) ror, mir - ror on the wall, act - ing like it knows it all.

Don't be shy, don't be scared, you don't
Tells you lies of van - i - ty, it does-

Nobody Ever Told You - 8 - 1

ONE WAY TICKET

Words and Music by
CARRIE UNDERWOOD,
JOSH KEAR and LUKE LAIRD

Moderate reggae feel ♩ = 80

(Whistle)

mf

1. If you're tired___

Verse 1:(sing first time only)

of your life and the way that you feel,___ like a fish on a hook, like a bug on a dirt-y wind-

Verse 2:(sing second time only)

up your smile and your new flip flops, we're head-ed to a heav-en where the beat don't___ stop.___

62

Chorus:

One Way Ticket - 7 - 3

64

66

One Way Ticket - 7 - 7

THANK GOD FOR HOMETOWNS

Words and Music by
ASHLEY GORLEY, LUKE LAIRD
and HILLARY LINDSEY

Moderately ♩ = 104

(with pedal)

Verse 1: (Sing first time only)

1. Yes-ter-day__ I got a call,__ some-one I did-n't know at all

Verse 2: (Sing second time only)

(2.) June my cous-in tied the knot,__ did-n't know if I__ would go or not,__ but

had passed__ a-way.__ Ma-ma said,__ "Yeah, you know him,__ you went

I'm sure glad__ I__ did.__ It was a pret-ty good haul, but worth the drive.__ I could

Thank God for Hometowns - 7 - 1

71

Thank God for Hometowns - 7 - 5

GOOD IN GOODBYE

Words and Music by
CARRIE UNDERWOOD,
HILLARY LINDSEY and RYAN TEDDER

Moderately slow ♩ = 84

Verse 1:

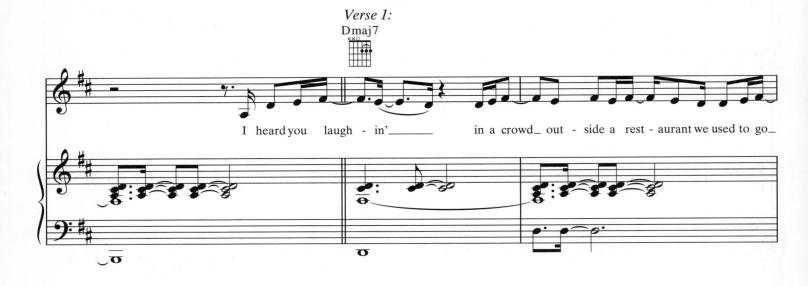

I heard you laugh - in'_____ in a crowd_ out - side a rest - aurant we used to go_

___ to. I caught a glimpse that stopped_me_ in my tracks, it took_ me___

* Original recording in D♭. Guitars tuned down 1/2 step.

78

80

LEAVE LOVE ALONE

Words and Music by
HILLARY LINDSEY, GORDIE SAMPSON
and TROY VERGES

Moderately, with a slight country swing ♩ = 88

Verses 1&2:

1. Fun-ny how love__ can make you feel,____
(2.) fun-ny how love__ can make you fly,____

Leave Love Alone - 7 - 1

84

just can't leave love a - lone, hey.

2. Ain't it

Come on.

Bridge:

86 *Chorus:*

Leave Love Alone - 7 - 6

CUPID'S GOT A SHOTGUN

Words and Music by
CARRIE UNDERWOOD,
JOSH KEAR and CHRIS TOMPKINS

A7

Bb7

Turns out I'm too hard to hit,__ so he

I'm dug down in my fox - hole, wait - in' on__

put a - way__ his bow.__ I might just keep on

__ his next__ bar - rage.__ Must be o - pen

run - nin' from here__ to Tim - buk - tu.__ 'Cuz

sea - son, got__ a tar - get on__ my__ back.__

94

WINE AFTER WHISKEY

Words and Music by
CARRIE UNDERWOOD,
DAVE BERG and TOM SHAPIRO

Moderately slow ♩ = 66

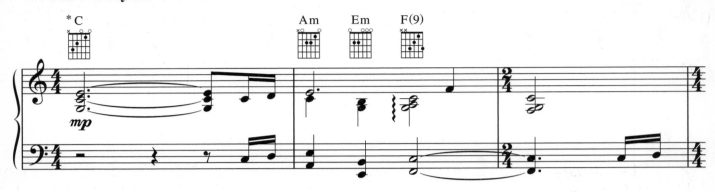

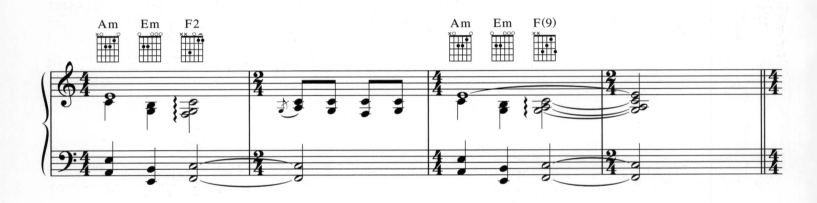

Verse 1:

1. Once up-on a time our world was on___ fi - re,_____ and I

* Original recording in D♭ major, guitar Capo 1.

Wine After Whiskey - 6 - 1

WHO ARE YOU

Words and Music by
R.J. "MUTT" LANGE